COLC

Carol Watson and Heather Amery
Illustrated by David Higham

Consultant: Betty Root
Centre for the Teaching of Reading
Reading University, England

This is Mr Bonk, the toymaker. He makes all kinds of wooden toys.

No one wants to buy them so he is very sad.

One day his friend Leo, the artist, comes in with some big cans of paint.

"Why don't you paint your toys bright colours?" he says. "Then everyone will want them."

Mr Bonk opens a can of paint. The colour inside is red.

"What shall we paint red?" he says.

"A fire engine is red," says Leo.
"Let's paint this one."

Can you think of other things that
might be red?

Leo opens another can. "This is blue," he says.

So they paint some of the toys blue.

6

Which toys are blue?
Which toys are red?

Which toys are blue and red?

Another can has yellow paint in it.
Lots of things are this colour.

Bananas and daffodils are yellow.
What other things are this colour.

"Let's paint the doll's hair yellow,"
says Mr Bonk.

"And her shoes," says Leo.

Mr Bonk looks out of the window.
He sees the fields and trees.
"Let's paint something green
like the grass and leaves," he says.

"We don't have any green paint," says Leo. "But we can make it."

He puts yellow paint and blue paint on a plate and mixes them.
"Hey presto, now we have green paint," he says.

Mr Bonk and Leo paint some of the toys green.

How many green toys can you see?

Find the blue toys, then the red and the yellow ones.

Which toys are two colours?

One can has white paint in it.

"This is not really a colour," says
Leo. "But we can use it to make
other colours."

He mixes some red paint with some white paint.

"You have made pink," says Mr Bonk. "That's just right for the doll's face."

The last can of paint is purple.

"Not many things are this colour,"
says Leo. "Can you think of any?"

"Some flowers are purple," says Mr Bonk. "And some fruit," says Leo.

Can you think of anything else that is a purple colour?

"I've mixed red and yellow paint," says Mr Bonk, "and made one more colour."

It is orange.

They painted the rest of the toys with his colour.

Do you have anything orange?

Everything has been painted with lots of different colours.

Can you remember all their names?

How many different colours did Mr Bonk and Leo use?

Can you think of any other colours?

Now the toys are such bright colours all the children want them.

Mr Bonk is very happy.

Colour mix
Can you remember which colours
Leo made when he mixed
these paints?

First published in 1984
Usborne Publishing Ltd
20 Garrick St, London
WC2 9BJ, England
© Usborne Publishing Ltd 1984

The name of Usborne and the
device 🎈 are Trade Marks of
Usborne Publishing Ltd.

Printed in Portugal